Wall Clock

Shane McLaughlin

BookLeaf
Publishing

10
Unidades

WALL CLOCK

Shane McLaughlin

Presentation by *BookLeaf Publishing*

Web: www.bookleafpub.com

E-mail: info@bookleafpub.com

ISBN: 9789357448352

First edition 2022

DEDICATION

For the reader...

ACKNOWLEDGEMENT

Everyone whom I'd like to thank is dead. So I'd like to give spotlight acknowledgements to Ludwig Wittgenstein, Anne Sexton and Emil Cioran.

PREFACE

These poems take inspiration from strange points, make-believe scenarios that run amuck in the author's head, and from lovers. So everything. These poems were inspired by everything.

Paper Flight

I write myself to life;
The last flight of a
Broken-winged bird.
I resuscitate sounds
Thought to be long forgotten;
The rise of the never-dead.
She makes beauty seem repulsive;
She tells me pretty words to
Trick me into verse.
The living breath of me
Swelling up and down
After each line.
So long as these papers
Never burn,
I'll never die.
(I wrote myself a tombstone)
I write myself to life.

House-Bound

There are terrible people,
There are good ones too.
I pretend I know the difference
and write each
poem as a dirge, each
letter as coin over my eye
so that I'm richest in death.
Swing sets off set
The turbulence of
Loving someone and then
realizing you haven't the
damndest idea what you mean
by that.
So you spend years in
a slow globe, in
the paradigmatic house,
hermetic, walls dancing
with family portraits.
You love until you're mad.
Kids imprint the floor,
floorboards grow
timorous and frail,
collecting years
and dust and calcium.
O skeleton, my wife,

your kisses are dry.
O kids, you'll have
to care for this loosening
skin. You're taut and young.
I'm but a mark on a page.
I hope this all goes away.
Does that make me terrible?
I'm unsure why I thought this
was a good idea.

parole

Your whole heart in my
Hand,
Beating like a headache.
I
Find deserts overbearing
I
Cannot think about
The
Things you say, because
You
Say them most perfectly.
And
It scares me that breath
Can
Give rise to arms, to
Movement,
To death and all her
Languished
Birds. Your heart evacuates,
Loosens,
Becomes sand; it spills between
My
Fingers, my celestial fingers
That
Once held yours.

Away,
You fall,
Away,
You always fall
Away,
Come back, I
Miss,
The flow of your words,
Your
Waves breaking upon
Mine.

Apocalyptic Analysis

The bread finds a liking towards being stale; and
the pantries can be harvested for dust, beyond
which it's pointless.
The neon signs ask kindly for the vines to
retract; and diners slouch languished under the
weight of the sun and the clicking water.
The graveyards hardly look different; grass
stalks tall as bonedogs; trees wrapped in earth's
green varicose veins; infantries of
moss-sweatered stones.
Scrapers lay horizontal like cancer patients
bed-bound; and cars wear the slippers of brush
and concrete.
Street lamps like a buckled leg; glass planted
into the ground with the prospect of becoming a
see-through tree.
Linoleum curling to break free from dormancy;
walls broken in and straining to keep up the
weight.
Here or there a hole brimming with bones; they
whisper silent chitters to delight the dirt with
tales of death.

6 foot down and counting, burying itself, dying
for the second, third, fourth…
If a bird calls it's only to ask to be spared.
The lively world of trash walking with aid from
the wind.
A scab of star-shaped black at random intervals;
shrapnel and bullet shells cubbied by sidewalks
and shop fronts.
If a human called, he wouldn't.
Blood graffitied onto whatever would have it.
Obsolete campaign posters; nature won by a
landslide.
A raped cash register.
An explosion of still cars.
The streets are stop-motion, but to never be
picked up again.
Ask around and no one will tell you.
A fence of heads on a suburban lawn.
If a dog barked it would be its last.
Golden-backed butterflies flicker.
And I wonder if things will be any different than
they were before.

Sleep

when you turn off the lights
and crawl into bed, I
think about what it's like to die.
every night.
and it scares me
because my eyes get variegated
marks and soft remembrances
of the outline of the lights, then it
goes black,
and then I feel like crying;
and I feel you're there with me,
but I feel like I'm slipping away,
and I want to shake you awake
and kiss you,
but I can't tell you that I'm dying
every night as I fall asleep; I can't explain
that sort of thing to you.
then I worry that if I don't,
I'll die alone.
so I tell you, and you call me silly
and brush my hair and kiss me again.
then I want to die
there,
asleep,
with you.

Sicknesses

You are sick
with
dreams.
You believe the
evening shakes,
that the sun sets
for you,
only you.
Untrue.
Your ears
are sick
with flies,
they hum,
they tell
you stories
of
dead dogs.
Days carry
pathogens,
sicknesses
that grow
out of your
bed.
Your hands are sick,
vein-riddled,

a poetic mess,
stained with
bruises,
purple
scars like
lilacs.
Maybe you
need a doctor,
"a diagnosis
with legs."
Maybe you
need it beaten
out of you.
Maybe
a moonbeam
will scare
the sickness,
or maybe
we can make it
our friend.

Ode to a Smoker

I always breathe in your smoke.
Tired squeaks of wheels
touching concrete,
rain clinging onto leaves,
windows growing
lumpy with water.

Jesus himself - that is what you inhale.
And out disperses the Holy Spirit.
I breathe him in and cough,
menthol tingling my lungs.

The dash's dull gloss,
a cubby to keep your lighter in.
Air fresheners are like
breath mints for your car.

And the radio doesn't sing,
your ears are attuned to silence.
The engine doesn't hum.
And the crackling of
tobacco and paper
is the only music you like,
for I always breathe in
your smoke.

My coughing is the
rhythm you burn your song to.

parenthetical

She said she (once)
loved me.
That we would (wouldn't)
make it.
How the sun opened (closed)
its lazy eye on us.
Always (never)
did the months pass by.
Singing (crying)
at me.
Playing (fighting)
in messy kitchens.
She would (wouldn't)
always (ever)
be mine.
So we sanctified (roiled)
beds.
So we kissed (bit)
one another,
skin a sweet (sour)
thing.
So snow would fall (melt).
Time would pass (ache).
Bodies would mature (desiccate).

And we would always love (hate)
one another.
Like gods (mortals).
Like lovers (nothing).

Day 9

You look so good in nothing,
by nothing i mean your
skin,
by your skin i
mean your shape,
all pressed against
the crying wall,
the house screams
for you;
but nothing touches you
(save me)
only pluming breath,
hands holding like adhesive,
sounds like falling angels.
and when you shed
your skin, let
no soul reprise.
let no love
go unanswered.

Untitled

I've ripped another sliver
Of flesh off my finger, and
Blood is starting to cumulate
In a groove and spill onto
My nail.
It hurts, but I take
Another bite and tear deeper
Until a recess of epidermis begins
To spurt plasma and red.
I put the red finger in
My mouth and taste iron.
It's good.
I have a trash bag full
Of manuscripts and poems,
And I want to bite so deep
Into my skin that maybe
Instead of blood, words
Will come out.

Wall Clock

At twelve a.m. the night passes through a malicious fit of melancholy that eats away the hour as some insomniac realizes his torment, coming to terms with another sleepless night with his head plastered in his pale hands, holding his frowny face that happens to not be his but the face of everyone else.

At one a.m. the night falls back into itself, realizing the next day, yet dazed as it still lingers in the dark, waiting for the fiery sun that smiles over the cool evergreens at the break of dawn, where workers toil; and the night wallows with this as, instead, it burns a hole in the heart of some sleepless poet composing the proverb of love to win over the coy girl who daydreams in class.

At two a.m. the moon dances as the ocean's ebb crescendos out the window of a decrepit hut that houses a witch who, with a stoical joy, whispers incantations over the body of a dead animal that was her life long companion as she strokes its soft fur and as her eyes fill with sorrow, dripping out one by one the tears of the poet and the insomniac who are still awake, maddened by the hour.

At three a.m. the ghosts, ghouls, and goblins alike pass out of their world and into ours, passing the witch and the poet and the insomniac, bidding them a good-night as their transcendental bodies traverse the plain of madness and hate that teems through the earth like a bee's hive, shrouding the mostly sleeping world with dreams. The frightening shapes of evil are really not so deplorable at this hour, seeing as how they, like the poet, are poignant at heart, and they, like the insomniac, are driven to be by a force out of their control, and are oddly enough made dormant by virtue of their being but not in the sense that they are immobile; rather, they cannot change their pathological makeup that condemns them to the steely carapace.

At four a.m. the first glints of light spread through a pasture next to the flower bedecked hills that yawn endlessly, as the shepherd, too, stretches his arms, then makes breakfast for strength to continue working on the pasture, fending off the wolves who, as we know, are beasts; leaving us to look towards the poet who is asleep at his desk with a stubby pencil resting in his hand, shortened by the long verse composed with verve that sat sad on his desk, lifting and drooping with the breeze that floods through the window.

At five a.m. the workers have finished
drinking their steamy coffee and are now
swinging a wooden axe at the evergreens who
scream with each virulent hack as another great
elder - much older than the man who cut him -
falls with a harrowing crash onto the plushy
grass of the wet forest; leaving us to queue in on
the witch who, with the same stoical joy, hangs a
noose from the splintered rafters, then takes the
leap into her next life to join her friend who has
been dead now for some time and who's buried
in the graveyard next to the advancing ocean,
walking through the realm that houses not the
worst of mankind but the most pitiful.

At six a.m. some lifeless worker steps out
of bed, hopping into his pants with both legs to
feel the jubilance of uniqueness, continuing then
to sneer when a large woman passes him or
when an ugly girl steals a glance; yet as this
happens the insomniac still sits with his head
cradled in his hands, staring blankly at the wall.
When the former starts towards work, having
made a jest of the world around as he passed it
by, feeling himself unequalled as he pretends the
pit in his soul is satiated by his cunning which is
really a repugnance or miasma that seeps
through his loathsome pours, excreting the
effluvium of abhorrence, he punches in ten
minutes late.

At seven a.m. the sun looks to be resting on
the pinnacle of a mountain, not smiling but
seething as another tree topples to the ground,
followed by the malignant sounds of wolves
catching sheep, followed by the tireless squeak
of the taut rope hanging the witch and the deep
staccato of the poet's snoring. Nothing great
happens at seven save the insomniacs
movement, which is the shifting of hand to head
as he frowns seriously into the wall that might as
well be an abyss, but nothing stares back.

At eight a.m. the world is awake, bustling
with life as cars shred down the highway and
banks fill with stodgy folk that abide by the
dollar bill, taking care to be just selfish enough
to keep themselves miserable but satiated, unlike
the contentedness that is impossible for the six
o'clock worker to reach, seeing as how now, at
this fine hour, he is serving breakfast to a quaint
woman with scraggly hands who is trying to
produce the exact change for a purchase as he
sighs into her face the obstinate sigh of someone
who believes they are destined for better but are
unwilling to do a paltry kindness by helping the
sedulous woman who looks upon her reluctant
succor and eventually gives up as the worker
tells her not to worry about the change.

At nine a.m. the witch arrives in the next
world that looks to be nothing but is everything,

only too close to be seen and amalgamated into such a perfect union that sees its significance in not being an identifiable something but an obscure nothing that sits veiled in black like a stone on a mantlepiece that a child might awe at, having never seen such a dark color that both reveals himself and everyone else, that houses both the witch and the world he breathes in.

At ten a.m. there's nothing left of the evergreens save their derelict stumps that are desiccating under the odious sun who once gave them life but is now stealing it away like the insomnia that stole the man's sleep or how the coy girl stole the poet's heart or how god stole the witch's familiar or how caprice stole the six o'clock worker's happiness; all the while the lumberjacks realize it was themselves who took away their work, cutting what they thought was an infinite forest. And now, they are taking their axes to another forest to cut one last tree to whittle a hungry gallows that swallows their pates with its bristly rope. Their bodies then rot into a diaphanous paste slowly from their bones as the sun cracks a mirthless smile then reverts back to a grimace realizing it wasn't karma that killed the workers but him with his virulent rays.

At eleven a.m. the wall clock stops and so does the rest of time as the world freezes over ephemerally; then, as the clock is fed new batteries, time begins anew, writhing about the air unseen like a mote; swimming fervently about into the rooms of the poet and the insomniac, it lands neatly on poet's head, waking him with a gasping breath as he rips the poem off his desk and runs out into the day with only one heavenly thought which is of his coy soul-mate who has practically waited until death for her fastidious composer who guides the pencil not with his hand but with his heart as hours engulf the wall clock that watches over him as he writes in his dormant pocket of time.

At twelve p.m. a meteor falls onto the yawning wasteland of the desert, seen by no one as it burns tirelessly in the sand, crying, not because it was injured, rather, because there was no one there to witness its beautiful landing onto the moor of his new home - his home until the universe implodes, reverting everything back into that milky black stone.

At one p.m. the world is on fire, scorching the workers till they're a solid block of soot that sunders from the midline in the baking light like an egg cracked into a bowl; but instead of a yolk, a charred heart falls from the crevice of their chests onto the lava floor that envelopes the organ in a red hot molasses. All the while the lumberjack's bodies are being buried by the stumps; their remains left to be exhumed by the curious foxes that roam the forest wasteland.

At two p.m. the poet has just left the gray subway and is going up steep steps towards the taunting sun that once more smiles upon seeing the fervor of the hustling poet, who then reaches the dilapidated apartment complex on the outskirts of the linear city, walking breathlessly up a few more steps, trepidatious and shaking as his fist now touches the door with a few dull thuds, followed closely by the scrapping of feet and the unlatching of a door.

At three p.m. the world ends. Not really, but symbolically as it is too late and too early to do anything, leaving the sulking insomniac with the tedious task of scrutinizing his wall as the sun begins to topple over the other side of the sky, blaring hot air at the faces of the downtown denizens who are huddled together, packed in tight like sardines, holding tenaciously onto their wallets lest it should be swiped to provide just enough money for one weeks worth of food to some thief who isn't really a thief but a human, corned both by his consciousness and the crowd surrounding him.

At four p.m. the world is depressed, and the sun frowns as the day feels like it is coming to a close and begins to falter in the blue sky as the population looks languished upon their wall clocks that are really a time prison keeping them caged but by nothing corporeal. Nothing happens at four save the insomniac's mirthless smile that easily wipes away as he crawls into bed, depleted but failing to fall asleep.

At five p.m. a tumult rises from a neon bar situated on a dark corner, congested by the abodes of washed out nobodies who, in that moment, are actually somebodies as they flee their feeble lives to entertain their lust for companionship, like the poet who is united with his lover, having vocalized the aphorism of his love to her clever face as she takes his hand in hers, rubbing the knuckles of the pompous boy, then placing one soft kiss on his cheek that burns like the smiling sun.

At six p.m. a feast is brought out for the affluent who do not eat their rations but drink their bloody wine, red from the sore fingers of the restless workers who are satiated by the bread that is both hard and old, realizing they are not happy, yet they aren't poor, not while they hug their sallow families and not while they're friends with the house mice who come out to share their evening meal as they wrap their wounds together granted they should heal before the next day's toil, where their hands will not only be cut and bruised, but torn from their arms

by the maws of the glutenous fat man who
hadn't enough to eat at the prior night's dinner.

At seven p.m. the sun cries, but instead of
tears, a pink and blue tinge hangs over the heads
of the tired people who, if they aren't home,
they're out with friends, dancing for the moon to
come up save the upheaval of life should don on
them like the insomnia that enlightens the man
who has taken up his seat again in front of the
vanilla wall that eludes its secrets, only teasing
its tail like the foolish rabbit just quick enough
to hop away, lest it should be swallowed whole
by the affluent who is not really rich, but insane,
as he scampers towards the sun, trying to evoke
an emotion that has long been hidden like a
trove.

At eight p.m. the sun recedes behind the
mountain range as the glowing moon, veiled in
white, dapples striated beams onto the
smoldering meteor who has lost all will to exist,
so it holds its breath granted all oxygen should
evacuate his lungs. But as he does this, a ghostly
witch, bewildered and lost, sprints down the
dune's crest, tumbling down, down, only to
come upon the milky black meteor, who is really
a cosmo, and hug it to death.

At nine p.m. the night secrets a hollow
moan that echoes through the heart of the poet as
he sits beneath an oaken tree, staring up upon

the glistening stars who do not dance but freeze
as all light discontinues its movement for just
one moment, letting the young man's heart fill
with a molten metal that solidifies the boy into
statue, imbedded with words and suffused with
forever golden innards as he later becomes the
symbol for love and serenity, construed to have
meaning as all things need meaning.

At ten p.m. everyone is asleep save the
scattered few with copious maladies that allows
meaning to pass over them like the dream that
comes over all, the glorious one where they are
no longer frightened of death but welcome it
cordially like an old friend, except this friend is
perhaps more ancient than death, but isn't life as
there is a surmounting nexus that connects the
two desolate terms to form an aggregation, not
to serve a purpose but to be exactly what it is: a
nothing that is everything - a face that frowns;
the torsioned visage of a contradicting clown.

At eleven p.m. the world ends, this time for
real, as reality cracks from the screen that is
really the medium between your eyes and the
page, like a cement wall bashed with a heavy
hammer which is gripped in the hands of the
witch and the poet and the six o'clock worker
and the affluent and the meteor and the quaint
old lady and everybody as everything crumbles
to nothing, reverting back into its primordial

form: that of a milky black stone: dense, mad and absolute.

At twelve a.m. the insomniac looks up towards his wall clock and sighs, noticing it's only been a few minutes.

expiate and prayer

You can exhaust paper,
Butcher a million trees,
And still have said nothing.
Blood can be rushing from
Your fingertips, bibles can be
Splayed open, windows
Follying the wind; and, still,
Your words are simply debilitated.
It's terrible to write because
You never know when the
Wellspring will dry. You never
Know if ideas are self-replenishing.
You simply pray the words don't
Age, that water never condensates,
That pain can always relieve itself
So long as it's turned to, say, a
Snarling poem.

One has no God;
But if one did they'd
Pray for
Inexhaustibility.
The prayer:
Hail sadness, full of charm,
Never leave me; blessed art

Deaths among loved ones;
And blessed is the
Prospect of my own, the poem.
Stay with us writers now
And so long as we care.
Amen.

Princess of Death

They don't remember
The sonnet or their first
Love, or the combination
To the smiles you've
Long locked away.
You see yourself
On the street, in tears,
Fairies and dead rats
Swirling around you.
O princess of the dead,
You look tired today.
It's not easy taking life
When yours is the
Only one you wish
Would go away.
In harming yourself
You harm everyone else.
Stabbing your skin
Like an unwanted apple,
But what breaks away are
Mountains.
Once you find a way
To kill yourself,
I know we'll all go with you
To someplace better.

Where it always snows
And light always melts
Against the ground.
Where instead of rocks
Or birds or cities,
You see red, at last,
Streaming through
Your veins.

resting place

Is loving
Being owned?
Are stars askance
To the moon?
Perhaps I can't speak,
Perhaps writing
Should be left
To anyone
Else.
I am soft-spoken,
An unrepresented metaphor,
Bridled and safe.
Perhaps I should take
My medicine.
Perhaps I should
Cry.
Your absence does
Not assume silence.
May my thoughts not
Be too loud
For my voice.
May friends stop leaving.
May the flowers
Stop speaking.
Perhaps I am mad.

Perhaps let's stop
While we're ahead.
May these poems get
Somewhere;
May they take
Your hand and
Guide you
To your resting place.

Day 3 (cont'd)

stay,
can't the graveyard wait?
i want you for a time
equivalent to forever.
your hair reminds me
of the trees that
protect the birds.
stay,
for i have welcomed
you into my heart.
don't run when you
see the scars,
the match marks that
make up my hands.
why wouldn't i
kill the body to
free the soul?
but stay.
i have stories like
unwatered house plants.
i can repeat myself
until my voice annoys you.
then i'll write for you.
until the fracture parts fatally.
until lakes are swallowed

up by fish.
stay until we can both
rest in the dirt,
bone remarking bone.
and in the depths of
nothing i'll
never stop
looking for you

Color-Blind

Dark as a closed mouth,
the room is dark as a
closed mouth.
The TV salivates and
deteriorates you
into images.
Your two eyes are
screens,
deadly,
inscrutable.
Time blankets you
in sameness.
These walls grow
dim,
nothing satisfies your
craving for nothing.
Dear thoracic dinners,
eating only
to stay watching.
Color leaves your face,
dark as a closed mouth.
spitting up blood,
spitting up laughter,
spitting up teeth;

shallow black and white.
Memories flake
off your skin.
Wedding belts melt,
melt like hot flesh.
Dazzling and blind;
static makes
up your pupils.
And when you die
you'll walk back
into the TV's
window.

the ground yearned
for the sky

Children as
loose as gravel;
mothers pulling
their tearful earrings;
fathers engaged
with the
importance-of-today.
Who cries at the stains
they leave behind?
Thinking now it must
all be uprooted and
thrown away.
But love is a stain;
and how you
try your best to
scrub it away.

I see angels in
the groove of
sidewalks;
plumes of holy
seems to hood

your face.
I cannot wish
the seed to grow;
one must first
cry onto it.

And now you
make sense
in false light;
all your blemishes
like unbitten apples.

And are we just
scathings on
the earth?
Or maybe
the earth
wishes the moon
to kiss it?
Or maybe
you were that moon;
and I was merely
gravel and those
tears didn't
seem important
that day.

rhetoric of space

The chair is
An an unhad repose;
The couch sits
The council of
Water-logged thoughts;
The fan grants
Oxygen and molecular
Excitement so
That you're cooled.
The TV is a stagnant
Motion, a long flash, a
Deepening hollow;
Stairs ascend, ascend,
If climbed high enough,
To another world,
Each a perfect next, tip tap
Tip tap;
The bookcase is a universe,
A balling galaxy, an end
And beginning.
For the clock is a puzzle -
Shifting moments
Forward, occupying
An odd position in space,
Suspended, timed-out;

For the stove is
Hell simulated, nothing
Much lives there-about;
For the window
Deceives, a crystal
Clear lie.
And of the tea pot? -
Farce.
Of the cabinets? -
Out-of-commission dimensions.
Of the fridge? -
Microcosmic reenactments.

The dog is a slab of
Cogs and locomotion -
Steaming, heaving, panting.

What could a wife be? -
A meek incubator?
And children? -
Paltry analogs
Making messes,
Unraveling the
Continuum?

We smash this all
Together and call
Ourselves "happy"?

betterment

Things, I promise,
Things will get better.
Not every poem
Laughs at you.
Not every look
Is a gunshot.
You are simply
Frail,
Frail as
A loving look,
Dying behind
Everyone's back.
To be seen; but you are small.
To be heard; but you are quiet.
To be loved; but you are taken
By thoughts that won't let go.
You etch these words softly.
You are scared the paper
May wake up and swallow
These markings.
So maybe you are
Like a graveyard,
Leaving dead words
In your attic on
Sere page;

But maybe at the close
Things will be okay.

moral quandary

You have
The opportunity
To say something,
Something important.
You can appeal
To armies but
You're content
With dust.
You can speak oceans
But you are
Satisfied with puddles.
Here, right here,
You can make angels bow;
But you merely bite
Your fingers bare.
You prioritize
Flowering wounds
And sickness;
For health is
A luxury you can't afford.
Here you pray to no
God, just to the
Sheet to receive these
Words well. You
Have no form; you

Are bodiless.
You have no authority;
These lines are
Are breakable as hearts.
You have no meter,
Just a hunger for
Speaking.
You can better the world;
Yet, you'd rather see it in
Tears.
To let eyes saturate in ink,
Hands to tremble
With semblance.
Hearts to fill with what? -
Sadness.

i can't remember waking up

The way you say
"I love you"
Sleeps heavily
Across my chest.
I heave to hear you
Say it, dark lips, cut
From sun-stained
Clouds.
I think of you
When I kill flowers.
Did you know
I thought of you
At all?
From window sills
Marching with possibilities,
And you choose me?
If you left I'd take it
Terribly.
Probably destroy every article
Of you and hang
On loosely
To poems I bled

Onto.
Your sigh burns.
Your distance pulls.
Your eyes kill.
I broke the water fountain
Because I didn't want
Anyone else
Drinking after you.
Slurring calls, cries,
Streets pumping with
Heat waves, streetlights
Lonely to never share
Their neighbor's light.
We walked. Didn't speak.
Just stepped. And I won't
Say that I felt like your
Silence said a million words,
Because your silence
Just felt like silence.
But I like the quiet,
To hear the departure
Of top lip from bottom,
An airplane taking off.
Your heart was beating so loud.
And in the ether of heat,
I heard every organ tick; and
Your mouth split and said
"I love you."
I can't remember waking up.